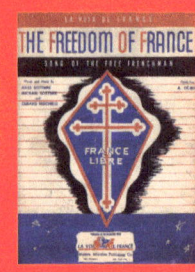

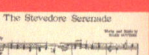

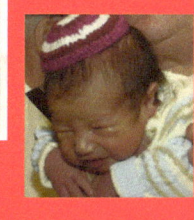

surviving

Akira Ohiso   Ellie Ohiso

zinc plate press

With much appreciation to....

Boaz Jules Ohiso
Mom & Dad Ohiso
Mom & Dad Fertig
Judith Sloan
Mayer Fertig
Rabbi Aryeh Gotlieb

©2008 Akira Ohiso & Ellie Ohiso. All rights reserved. Photography and design by Ellie Ohiso. Photography from Ellie and Akira's wedding © Jonathan Gati Photography. No part of this work may be reproduced by any means without the prior permission in writing from the publisher, except for brief passages and quotations in newspaper, magazine, radio, TV or online reviews.

Published by Zinc Plate Press. www.zincplatepress.com
1st Edition.

Cataloging-in-Publication Data is available from the Library of Congress

ISBN 13: 978-0-6152-4147-0

Printed in the United States of America

zinc plate press

For Zaydie

Simcha Bunim
5768

> *If a Jew didn't exist, an anti-semite would invent him.*

– Jean-Paul Sartre

The photographs of the kiddush cup (goblet) featured on these pages belonged to Akira's great-grandfather, Jules Sottnek. Jules escaped the pogroms of Czarist Russia during the early 20th Century and sought refuge in Brooklyn, New York. While he did everything in his power to escape his Jewish heritage for fear of persecution, he couldn't foresee his great-grandson, Akira Ohiso, finding his way back to Judaism, culminating in his conversion in the year 2003. Akira, a social work director, was born and raised in New York, a child of interracial parents. His mother is an Irish-Russian Jew, his father is a Japanese immigrant. He married Ellie, this book's designer, in September of 2004 and, under his chuppah, drank from Jules' kiddush cup, which had been hidden almost a century earlier and later found in a dusty Brooklyn basement.

Jules S. Sottnek

Head of Stevedoring Company Founded by Him in 1922

Jules S. Sottnek, sixty-one, president of the Jules S. Sottnek Stevedoring Company, Inc., 17 Battery Place, died yesterday at St. Peter's Hospital, Henry and Congress Streets, Brooklyn. He lived at 11 Eightieth Street, Brooklyn.

Born in Riga, Latvia, Mr. Sottnek came to New York in 1911. He established the stevedoring firm in 1922 after being associated with the United Fruit Company and the Moore-McCormack Steamship Company. Mr. Sottnek and Hans Isbrandtsen, president of the Isbrandtsen Steamship Company, 26 Broadway, sponsored a series of free band concerts in Bowling Green Park during the war for the enjoyment of the public. Among Mr. Sottnek's clubs were the Maritime Association of the Port of New York, the Propeller Club of the United States, Port of New York, the Downtown Athletic Club and the Foreign Commerce Club. Surviving are his wife, Margaret Sottnek; a son, Paul W. Sottnek, and a daughter, Mrs. Lester Stockard.

Jules S. Sottnek, Akira's Great-Grandfather

1911 — Jules escapes the pogroms in Latvia, comes to NY with kiddush cup.

1922 — Jules founds the Jules S. Sottnek Stevedoring Ship Company, Inc.

1947 — Jules dies at the age of 61. Kiddush cup is found in his basement.

1970 — Akira Ohiso is born to Kaethe and Hisaaki Ohiso in Flushing, NY on March 8.

*Akira Ohiso, as a baby,
Jules' Great-Grandson*

*Boaz Jules Ohiso, as a baby,
Jules' Great-Great-Grandson*

1978 — Ellie Fertig is born to Eileen and Aaron Fertig in Freehold, NJ on March 7.

2003 — Akira converts to Judaism, receives Jules' kiddush cup as gift from mom.

2004 — Akira and Ellie marry. Akira uses Jules' kiddush cup under chuppah.

2006 — Boaz Jules Ohiso is born to Ellie and Akira Ohiso in New York City on November 11.

AKIVA: YOU ARE JEWISH

I went back to finish college after a long and unsuccessful attempt at a music career. At age 18, visions of rock stardom and all its superficial benefits fueled my musical ambitions, but at 27 I was finding emptiness in music.

Gigging became Tuesday nights in empty bars where applause sounded like a three-legged horse. I had an epiphany one night at a club in New York City as I lugged 50 pounds of equipment into my car at two-thirty in the morning. "I cannot do this anymore." I knew it was time for a change.

I enrolled in Queens College. Back in college at age 27 was a challenge. Aside from getting my academic muscles back in shape, I also felt that I was up against time as I needed to get my degree so I could move on and find a meaningful career. I was sick of making ends meet and yearned for something more. This degree represented my adulthood, my future, and my happiness.

I soon made friends, got involved in my studies, and majored in art. But, strangely, I also found myself being drawn to all things Jewish. Not that Jews were unfamiliar to me. I grew up in a Long Island suburb with a Conservative and Reform synagogue. I had many Jewish friends, attended Bar and Bat Mitzvahs throughout junior high school, participated in the occasional Seder, and was immersed in a certain secular Jewish culture.

But at Queens College it was much different. I was noticing Jews who wore kippahs (skullcaps) every day and had strings hanging from their belts. I noticed young girls with long skirts and head-coverings thronged together between classes. I noticed Jews with prayer books praying in quiet corners away from the fast-pace of secular life. It was strange and intriguing.

In one of my classes, I spoke to a Jewish girl. After class, a friend said, "You're wasting your time, she's Jewish." I said, "What do you mean? I've dated Jewish girls before."

He laughed and said, "Dude, she's Orthodox, they don't date anyone but their own kind." I noticed that his remark was tinged with disdain. Sarcastically, he ended with "good luck" and walked away.

What did he mean, "They only date their own kind?" I grew up in a community where Jews mixed with non-Jews. I had Jewish friends who dated non-Jewish girls. Orthodox Judaism seemed strange, archaic, and provincial. I was utterly intrigued by what I perceived as a closed community. The more I could not understand, the more I wanted to.

It was at this time that I met a girl named Ellie in one of my studio art classes. In our first conversations, she told me her name was short for Elisheva, the biblical name for Aaron's wife and sister-in-law of Moses. I knew very little about the bible other than the basics I learned in my Methodist confirmation class over 14 years ago at the age of 13. With church attendance only on Christmas and Easter, God and religion were not an important part of my upbringing.

When I got to know Ellie, she fascinated me with her dedication, knowledge, and obedience to Jewish religious law. She would say blessings before and after eating a meal, she would kiss mezuzahs when she left kosher restaurants, and she would even say a blessing after relieving herself in the bathroom. She was reminded of and connected to her religion in everything she did. It still seemed very restrictive to me.

One time after a rainfall, as a rainbow arced across the campus quad, she said a prayer. This completely astounded me. There was a prayer for rainbows? She explained that Jewish law was not set up to restrict Jews, but to set them free. She told me that through set limitations, focusing on the important things in life could be freeing.

I needed to be set free. For so long, I struggled to find myself. I was aimlessly searching. I was lost.

Ellie began to bring in strange books like tractates of the Talmud, Ethics of the Fathers, and the Torah. We went to local kosher restaurants and I loved shwarma in a pita with Israeli pickles. At the local Jewish bookstore, I was amazed at the stacks of leather-bound books all dedicated to God and improving one's self. Young Jews were deep in thought as they sifted through ancient words, women with hats and children bought everyday items like mezuzahs and bisomim boxes to enrich their Jewish observance, and old bearded men spoke in Yiddish about things I wanted to understand. In some strange way, these people made me feel comfortable even though I had never before met them.

I learned that Judaism placed great importance on family and community. A childhood friend - a ba'al teshuvah - who returned to Judaism after many years said, "I love that you can go anywhere in the world where there are Jews and you always have a place to eat, pray, and sleep." I loved this sense of community. The feeling of acceptance and inclusiveness made me feel safe. I had to believe that Jews turned to each other over the millennia as the outside world turned to persecution, scapegoating, and anti-Semitism. I couldn't put my feelings in words because it was so utterly strange. It was a feeling I never had before. Judaism felt right.

As Ellie and I became closer, I started attending Jewish events at the college Hillel. I spoke to my Jewish friends who thought I was crazy for even considering converting to Judaism. "Dude, being Jewish sucks." I started going to synagogues in my neighborhood and talking to rabbis. What I soon realized is that by going to a Reform synagogue, in Ellie's eyes, I would not be Jewish enough. Not that she truly believed this. I know she wanted our relationship to work out, but she spoke a lot about her parents, her community and what they might think.

It soon became clear to me that within Judaism there was a lot of inner strife. I had Orthodox rabbis denigrate the Reform and Conservative movements and visa versa. One Orthodox rabbi said, referring to Conservative rabbis, "They throw a little holy water and they think they can make someone a Jew." I even had Conservative rabbis judging the Reform movement while they were being judged by the Orthodox movement. "We do not accept Reform conversions."

As I continued to learn about Judaism, I discovered that even within the Orthodox movement there were different levels or strains that separated Jews even further. It was all very confusing to me and I couldn't understand how you could be a Jew to some and not to others.

Ellie and I continued to date and deny the fact that there was this religious barrier between us. We had so much fun together, but knew that one day we would have to face the big Jewish elephant in the room.

I just thought, "What's the big deal?" How could a religion dictate two people's love for each other? We broke up once or twice, but soon realized that we were bashert (soul mates) and could not stand time apart. We were perfect for each other in every way except for this religious barrier between us.

Even after we graduated from Queens College, Ellie continued to hide our relationship from her parents. The terror of telling her parents she was dating a non-Jew was so acute that she had to talk with a therapist.

It made me very angry. I gave up studying Judaism for a while and just left it up to fate. We continued our relationship, but it was like we were living in a vacuum. The outside world moved along, as our relationship remained stagnant and in denial.

My parents and friends knew all about Ellie, but I was not allowed into her world. My parents loved Ellie and wanted our relationship to work, but could not picture an Orthodox family accepting a non-Jew into the family whether I converted or not. To them, Orthodox Jews were Tevye from *Fiddler on the Roof*. My Japanese father innocently believed that all Jews were good with money. Ellie's father called Asians "Orientals" and his first associations were of a harbor in Hawaii. They grew up with the World War II ideologies, and reconciling black and white seemed hard for them. I had to believe there was gray.

But my parents supported us. My mom would follow the kosher rules of not mixing meat and dairy. She would use disposable pans and plastic utensils so Ellie could continue to observe the kosher laws at our home. I was struck by my mother's intrinsic enjoyment of catering to Ellie's kosher laws. My father loved talking to Ellie about his Japanese heritage and Ellie lovingly obliged.

And I slowly started observing kosher laws as well. I gave up pork and shellfish, I only ate kosher meat, and I separated meat from dairy. When I went out with non-Jewish friends I ate salads and vegetables. From an Orthodox standard, I was far from observing Kashrut, but it was a start. And, more importantly, I started to understand the choices and challenges that go into observing such an ancient and sacred practice.

I truly loved it. I went to the supermarkets looking for Hekhshers (kosher certification.) "Wow, Oreos are kosher? Cool!" "Damn, Welch's Grape Juice is not!" On Sundays, I went with Ellie to Great Neck, a town nearby, that had a large religious Jewish population. We ate lunch at shwarma joints and I tasted kosher Chinese food. It tasted no different than non-Kosher Chinese food. We perused Judaica stores for books. I bought *To Be A Jew*, a transliterated Siddur, a small Chumash, and my first kippah.

I chose one of those funky Bukharian kippahs because Ellie told me many Sephardic Jews wore them. I considered myself a Sephardic Jew at this point, because, for one I was not Ashkenazi, and, for another, it felt nice to pretend. I also was a little nervous about wearing a regular kippah everyday because it made me a target for anti-Semitism. I could hedge my Jewishness with a more discreet kippah. I was learning what it felt like to be hated for doing absolutely nothing.

All those news stories about Jews getting beaten by roaming gangs of anti-Semites

I had an epiphany one night at a club in New York City as I lugged 50 pounds of equipment into my car at two-thirty in the morning.

"I cannot do this anymore." I knew it was time for a change.

started coming back to me. Then came thoughts of The Holocaust and the millions that died because they were Jewish. For the first time, I understood the everyday struggles of Israeli Jews and the State of Israel.

Suddenly being Jewish became very real. Did I want to become a Jew?

Being Jewish was in my blood. My blood suffered with all Jews. My blood suffered the destruction of the Temples and The Holocaust. My blood was Jewish enough that Hitler would have sent me to the gas chambers.

Orthodox rabbis continued to deny working with me. I tried being honest by telling them about Ellie and I tried saying very little, but it didn't make a difference. One Orthodox rabbi, not knowing about Ellie, told me to buy a black hat and start living in his community where he would make arrangements. For him, it meant turning a switch; for me, it was about a sincere spiritual journey.

I also spoke to a Reform rabbi and a Conservative rabbi and explained that Orthodox rabbis would not convert me unless I broke up with Ellie for at least a year. They laughed at the Orthodox rabbis and encouraged me to join their brand of Judaism, as if I was buying a car or a pair of shoes.

As I continued to immerse myself in Judaism, my mother started to drop hints of our family's past. One evening she showed me a silver cup that was her grandfather's. I asked her if he was Jewish.

She said "Yes." Suddenly, my mother's affinity for Ellie and her Jewishness made sense. My mother was feeling her Jewish roots. I was amazed. The silver cup was actually a Kiddush cup.

I was excited to tell Ellie, and she was amazed. At first, she thought I may not have to convert if my family's Jewishness was passed down matrilineally. It wasn't, but it didn't matter.

Now I had a mandate from God. Now I understood why I felt so Jewish even though everyone told me I was not. Now I understood this inexplicable connection to Judaism.

Being Jewish was in my blood. My blood suffered with all Jews. My blood suffered the destruction of the Temples and The Holocaust. My blood was Jewish enough that Hitler would have sent me to the gas chambers.

From then on there was nothing that would stop me from becoming a Jew.

Ellie sat down with her parents one Sunday evening and told them about me. She was surprised when her father simply asked, "Do you love him?"

"Yes," she said, tears streaming down her face from two years of pent-up silence. Her father said, "Well, the rest is details then."

There was no Jewish guilt, there was no sitting Shiva, there was only "Do you love him?" I was not surprised because parents who raised Ellie had to be wonderful and accepting people. They did not disappoint.

While her parents preferred we go for the Orthodox conversion "to avoid later difficulties," they did not pressure us and let us move at our own pace. Ellie and I participated in a six-month Judaism class through the Conservative movement that could lead to conversion. I completed the course and was converted in September of 2003. I asked her to marry me, in the parking lot of the local mikvah after my conversion. I could not hold back the tears as I told her she was the best thing that ever happened to me. It was also how I felt about Judaism.

In the following year, I moved into the garage apartment of my future-in-laws. They wanted me to live in an observant Jewish community where I could learn first hand about Jewish holidays, Shabbos, and what it meant to live as a Jew. It was the most important learning experience of my life. My language became peppered with Yiddish and biblical Hebrew sayings, I was talking about Israel and Jewish politics, and I was not ashamed to voice my opinions as a new Jew.

Her immediate family accepted me as a Jew, but not everybody did.

Some relatives felt that a Conservative conversion was not recognized by the Orthodox movement. It started with a phone call to Ellie stating that I was not Jewish and therefore should not get married unless I converted Orthodox. One relative called our future children "mamzers" (a Yiddish derogatory term that means bastard) and started telling the local Orthodox rabbis about our relationship. The relative even started calling other relatives to discuss "the goy."

Here I was, passionate and sincere about my Judaism, a recent convert, and Jews, the very people that were supposed to accept me, were telling me I was not a Jew. My personality, my kindness, my heart and soul did not matter because in their eyes I was not Jewish.

In the months that followed, Ellie and I stood our ground and decided that we would go ahead with the wedding without an Orthodox conversion. We knew some family members would probably boycott the wedding, but that was their problem. She accepted me and that was all that mattered.

Soon, a funny thing happened. I started talking to Ellie's 85-year old Zaydie, a Holocaust escapee from Hungary, and the patriarch of the family. He talked to me about Jewish survival. He lost most of his family and came to the United States alone and penniless. He was mugged his first day in America and remembers his silver buttons being plucked off his winter coat.

Zaydie did not have to say much because his love for Judaism and his people was so strong, that I immediately understood. To him, it was not about politics and judgment, but about continuing the Jewish people. His reaction to my Conservative conversion was sympathetic, but he explained that it was important to him and his family that I become a Jew in a way that respected them. Being Jewish to him was gut level - nothing less, nothing more.

He explained that he knew I was Jewish in my heart and soul, and, therefore, an Orthodox conversion was only the final step in my journey. He explained that it was now just a halachic issue that could be fulfilled, but should in no way denounce my previous Jewishness. He said, "Akiva, you are Jewish."

I felt much better and less defensive. I understood that there were things I could not possibly understand about being Jewish. This 85-year old Jewish man, the patriarch of his family, and a Holocaust escapee, knew just a little bit more about being Jewish. I could see why he was so adamant about protecting the sacredness of Judaism.

because he nearly lost it.

The weekend before my aufruf, I met a rabbi in the Catskills and sat before a bet din. This was an Orthodox rabbi that had pushed me away several times, but on my fourth attempt agreed to do my conversion. I learned that rabbis turn potential converts away three times to ensure the convert is sincere.

The bet din was easy. I was not nervous because I was confident in my Jewishness. There was no question in my heart and soul. I was a Jew.

A ritual circumcision was done to symbolize Abraham's Covenant. As the rabbis watched, a drop of blood was drawn. This ancient ritual connected me to thousands of years of Judaism. I thought of Ruth, the first Jewish convert. I thought of my great-grandfather who was forced to renounce his Judaism. One rabbi told me that converts were God's way of replenishing the lost Jewish souls of The Holocaust. Another rabbi told me that if you save one life you save the world. I felt like I was saving future Jews as I brought Judaism back to my family.

Finally, I dunked myself in the mikvah three times and said the bracha.

Baruch Ata Adonoy Eloheinu Melech Ha Olam Asher Kidishanu B'Mitzvotav Vitzivanu Al Ha T'Veelah.

While I was underwater, I cherished the silent moment. All the struggles, all the adversity, all the questioning of my Jewishness only prepared me for life as a Jew. I knew that now I would not only be judged by Jews, but non-Jews as well. As I came to the surface and saw the faces of three bearded men, I finally said to myself, "No one can take away my Jewishness. I am a Jew."

They gave me loud hearty "Mazel Tovs" and handshakes. I chose the name Akiva Micah Ben Avraham Aveinu. I signed the conversion document and walked out of the unfamiliar shul to my car. The three rabbis got in their cars and drove away, leaving me to process what just happened. I was standing in a strange parking lot, in a strange town, and, yet, after 34 years of living, I, for the first time, finally felt like I was home.

All those news stories about Jews getting beaten by roaming gangs of anti-Semites started coming back to me. Then came thoughts of The Holocaust and the millions that died because they were Jewish. For the first time, I understood the everyday struggles of Israeli Jews and the State of Israel.

Suddenly being Jewish became very real.

Did I really want to become a Jew?

This 85-year old Jewish man, a Holocaust escapee, knew just a little bit more about being Jewish. I could see why he was so adamant about protecting the sacredness of Judaism, because he nearly lost it.

It was not about politics and judgment, but about continuing the Jewish people...Being Jewish to him was gut level - nothing less, nothing more.

Remember when we went to your parents for a Shabbos (sabbath) in Long Island? I was walking to shul (synagogue) with you. As we waited to cross at a stop sign, two guys in a car pulled up, rolled down their window and yelled, **"You dirty Jew."** They sped off cursing me. Once on the Upper West Side, a man saw an Israeli flag button I was wearing, and said, "You Jews are the problem!" Oh, I'm the problem. I work as a social worker in New York City, I love my wife and family, I want to help make the world a better place. I'm the problem? This is the question Jews have been asking themselves for millennia.

of color, foreig

Jews by choice

adoptees. The

Who is a Jew?

I AM A SOCIAL WORKER AT A JEWISH ORGANIZATION IN NEW YORK CITY THAT WORKS WITH HOLOCAUST SURVIVORS.

Most of my clients are in their 80's. Like any older person, my clients are struggling with declining health, loss of spouses and friends, less activity, isolation and loneliness. The aggregate of losses is a common theme of this stage of life. But, my clients also have the added burden of the Holocaust. This piece compounds and complicates the aging process as survivors, like all older people, must begin to review their lives, reconcile disparate experiences, and find resolve by saying "I know," a sort of peaceful detachment and letting-go of all that came before. Erik Erikson calls this stage of life "Wisdom vs. Self-despair." If clients can find resolve they attain Wisdom, but if they can't they continue to live in Self-despair. Either way, the chickens come home to roost, so to speak.

My oldest client is 104 and my youngest

client is 67. This is important because the age at which the trauma was inflicted plays a vital part in how survivors are coping today. Wherever someone was in the ego maturation process, or life stage, is where many of the survivors got stuck and never grew past, emotionally and psychically.

Some survivors grew up in Germany, Austria, or Poland before the war, before the Nazi regime came to power. They pursued careers, raised families, and had all the trappings of a middle class existence. They had the good fortune to come into a world of the same lives they were leading. They had the opportunity to have stable, well-adjusted childhoods. For other survivors, at the age of 5, they witnessed the Gestapo gun down their mother or father, or drag them to some unknown, never to be seen again, or they ended up under the scalpel of Dr. Mengele.

THEIR INCEPTION WAS INTO A WORLD OF BLOOD, ANGER, HATE, AND CHAOS. THEY DIDN'T HAVE A CHANCE.

HEDA 79 YEARS OLD LIVES ALONE
BORN: LEIPZIG, GERMANY

Heda calls from Lenox Hill Hospital. She had a mild stroke. She lives alone in low-income housing. One of those 80/20 buildings that allots 20 percent of the apartments to low-income tenants, and 80 percent to the open market. I think it's great. It forces people with money to cohabitate with the poor.

As a 13-year-old girl, she witnessed the Gestapo pull her mother and father from her home, never to be seen again. From then on, she was basically alone. She remembers being fed flour soup in a makeshift hospital. She escaped with another girl who died by the river. She shivered in the snow and "tried to catch the flu so I could die."

She remembers "Nazi doctors" injecting needles in her spine; she says it was "malaria blood" and "mercury"; she befriended a "retarded boy" in a hospital and the next day he just disappeared; she performed sex acts for food and shelter; she was raped by Nazi soldiers; she worked in a brothel. These memories are scattered, elusive, but acutely felt, always lurking in the dark corners of her psyche like waves beating against her sanity.

Heda called frantically and said, "They are trying to control my life. I don't want to go."

Her doctor suggested a sub-acute rehab facility to recover. Heda needed concrete medical services to help her with her impaired gait and balance. She refuses to go. These are benevolent people she sees as evil.

"They are trying to control me."

"They are trying to take me to a place where I can't go home."

"They won't let me go."

She was right back in the dark cobble-stoned streets of Germany looking to give a blowjob for a piece of bread. The reckoning is well underway.

Leipzig was the site of Leipzig-Thekla, a sub-camp of Buchenwald concentration camp. It was used to house Jewish laborers during the war. When the United States infantry found the camp in 1945, SS guards locked 300 laborers in their barracks and set-fire to them. Those that tried to escape were shot.

In Gaza, Jews fight Jews. It makes me very sad. I am starting to understand what born Jews feel like. For me, a convert to Judaism, the first couple of years has been a sort of honeymoon. But as I live as a Jew, I understand that the odds are really stacked against us. No matter what people say, anti-Semitism is an elusive yet insidious phenomenon. I am realizing that no matter where Jews are in history they are scapegoats for the ills of the world. Today, it is Israel. If Israel did not exist, there would be another political or religious ideology to perpetuate the fault of the Jews.

I wonder how far removed we are from the Holocaust? Saddam Hussein killed thousands of Kurds. He killed thousands of his own people because they did not conform to his evil ideology. He could not tolerate dissenting opinions. Yet, most of Europe thought removing Saddam from power was not moral. Politics cannot be involved in the deliberations to save innocent people. Most would say politics is always part of the equation. Well, then people will continue to directly and indirectly kill innocent human beings. It might sound too idealistic and simplified to expect a universal idea of morality, to expect an international mandate for justice and truth, but what is the alternative? Managed justice? Like our healthcare system? A labyrinthine system of special interests and politics, where the end result is money?

SAM — 89 YEARS OLD — WIDOWER
BORN: BERLIN, GERMANY

Sam lost his wife in September 2003. He has been smoking Pall Malls since he was a teenager. I encourage him to smoke now because it is the only thing he enjoys in life.

His life is centered around habits...exacting peculiar habits that give meaning to his life. He tells me he collects pennies in a kitchen drawer and when he gets 25 cents he brings it downstairs to the supermarket and exchanges it for a quarter. He then uses the quarter to buy The Post. Why he doesn't use the pennies to buy The Post is a mystery. Perhaps he likes holding silver-colored money.

After Passover, the rabbi at his shul (synagogue) was selling boxes of Streit's matzoh for ten cents a box. Sam bought 25 boxes and has them stacked above his kitchen cabinets.

He eats one piece of matzoh for breakfast with a cup of coffee and a piece of cheese, and one piece for lunch with "wurst" and a can of beer. He uses the same plate, cup, and utensils for each meal. He washes the dish, sets it for the next meal, and then sits down in his armchair. He gets a kosher meal from Meals On Wheels and saves it for dinner.

He saves the leftovers in the fridge or freezer, stacking meals upon meals that he will never eat. The guy down the hall brings him herring from a kosher deli in Brooklyn. A woman upstairs brings him challah for Shabbos.

He says the rabbi performed his wife's funeral. Sam can't go to shul anymore on Shabbos (sabbath) because the bathroom in the shul is in the basement and he needs an elevator. The rabbi won't leave the key in the elevator on Shabbos. Sam says the rabbi is too religious.

He says kaddish every night by himself.

He won't sleep in his bedroom because it reminds him of his wife. Instead, he chooses to sleep in the guest room. Sam urinates in a hospital bottle and empties it in the morning. "I use a little alcohol to clean it out."

When the Weimar Republic was defeated by the Third Reich in 1933, there were 160,000 Jews living in the German capital city. As the Third Reich increasingly restricted Jewish rights, 80,000 Jews were forced to emigrate. 60,000 Jews were deported to extermination camps.

Dear Akira

Today is a day you may remember for some time and I wanted to give you my thoughts and blessings. Last week's parsha gives us a mitzvah called "Shiluach Ha-Kahn." We are commanded to not take away the eggs from a nest until we send away the mother bird so she not witness the loss of her offspring. It is a very unique mitzvah because it is one of only two mitzvot where Hashem tells us our reward for doing the mitzvah — a long life. It brought to mind a story I once read about the Japanese Ambassador to Lithuania during the height of the Holocaust in Europe. Mr. Sugihara arranged for exit visas for many Jews, mostly children, to escape to Japan. In fact, the entire Mir Yeshiva was sent by him to Japan and was almost the only Jewish school to survive the Holocaust. When asked why he risked everything for these Jewish children he said that he was required to do so because of a code demanding the safety of a bird fleeing its nest. The similarity to the mitzvah of "Shiluach Ha-Kahn" is striking.

Although Sugihara was fired for his efforts, I am certain his rewards have come from a higher place. The reward for "shiluach ha-kahn" is the same as the reward for the only other mitzvah that we know, that mitzvah is the commandment to honor one's father and mother.

There are so many great Torah scholars who have come out of the Mir Yeshiva that the effects of Mr. Sugihara's efforts more than demonstrate the power of a single individual of Japanese heritage to have a profound effect on the Jewish community. My hope and blessing is to see such greatness from you for I believe you have proven yourself capable of great compassion and wisdom. To have been able to help you put on tefillin for the first time, to sit next to you for Megillah, to see you use a prayer book that I helped bring into being — all have brought me great honor. But sometimes, you need not do anything to show respect to parents. Children think they have to meet expectations to please parents. Mostly, all they have to do is be themselves. I suggest that you look at your Japanese name from a Jewish perspective.

Akira may mean "bright" in Japanese, but in Hebrew, the root word is "yakar" — precious. That is not something you need to hope to achieve — you are already there. You are precious to your family, you are precious to Ellie and you have become precious to us. And because you are so dear and compassionate on the inside I am confident that it is in your soul. As Ellie learned the other day with coffee — you cannot tell from what something looks like — it's the sweetness within that matters. It is already within you. The honor that any parent seeks is always present when they see your soul. Your compassion — as was Sugihara's — fulfills the mitzvah of "shiluach ha-kahn" and "kibud av v'em" — honoring your parents. And I wish for you to indeed receive the Torah's stated reward of long life. This is my blessing for you on this day. Hold it dear as you build your own nest.

      Love Aaron

YOUNG ISRAEL OF OCEAN PARKWAY

הערלת נרות

הננו מאשרים שהאיש **אקירא אוהיסו** עיר ניו יורק

נתבריר בפנינו ביה דין חתומי מטה בקבלת ע[ול]

[חוקי] דת משה וישראל גסל ב"ד

מצות ובמילה ובטבילה במקוה כשרה ביום כד — שמים וערל

הרי הוא מגרי הצדק, ומהיום והלאה ישראל ו

בישראל **עקיבא אבה**

ולראיה על כל הנ"ל באנו על החתום ב

שנה חמשת ב"ד פה **עלנויל ניו יארק**

נאום:
ראום:
ראום:

YOUNG ISRAEL OF OCEAN PARKWAY

CONVERSION PROMISE

I, **AKIRA OHISO**, residing at
~~NEW YORK NY~~ do hereby promise and take an oath that I accept upon
[mys]elf the entire body of mitzvot, scriptural and Rabbinic (D'Oraitah and D'Rabbanan)
[as a] perquisite to my conversion to Judaism. I promise to live my life in accordance with
[To]rah-true, Orthodox interpretations and codifications of Jewish Law. My acceptance of
[all] the mitzvot, those I have learned as well as those yet unknown to me which I intend to
[le]am, is unequivocal and without reservation.*

I pray that G-d bless me with success. As proof of my intentions, I hereby sign
[th]is promise in the presence of witnesses.

NAME: **AKIRA OHISO**
DATE: **3/29/04**
PLACE: **ELLENVILLE, NY**

WITNESS
WITNESS

* This includes acceptance of and the strict observance of
1) Belief in One invisible G-d and rejection of any other religion
2) The yoke of the total mitzvah system (613), the scriptural and Rabbinic
3) The holy Shabbat including "tehum Shabbat," and muktza
4) Kashruth in and out of the house
5) The laws of family purity, Niddah, Mikvah, modesty and yihud
6) All the holidays, scriptural and Rabbinic (and Muktza)
7) Lighting candles (Shabbat and Holiday)
8) Netilat Yadayim, berakhot before and after eating
9) Being part of the Jewish People
10) Charity, love of Jews, love of Eretz Yisrael
11) Honesty, integrity, oaths and fulfillment of promises
12) Moshiah
13) Divinity of written and Oral Torah

בס"ד

נחנו ב"ד

שמר

בא לפנינו
בתוך נחנו
ובדיקות ע
שלם רצו
חוקי התור

על כן הוס
ולע

ויתנייר היו
עול
בפנ

ובטבילה
ויקרא שמו אב
אקיבא אבה בן אברהם אבי
ומהיום והלאה יש לו דין כו
צדק בישראל
וע"ד באנו עה"ח היום כ"ד אלול
פה עיר ע[לנוי]ל נו"י

נאום
נאום
נאום

What I realized when I was not Jewish is that the world is hyper-focused on what Jews are doing. Dennis

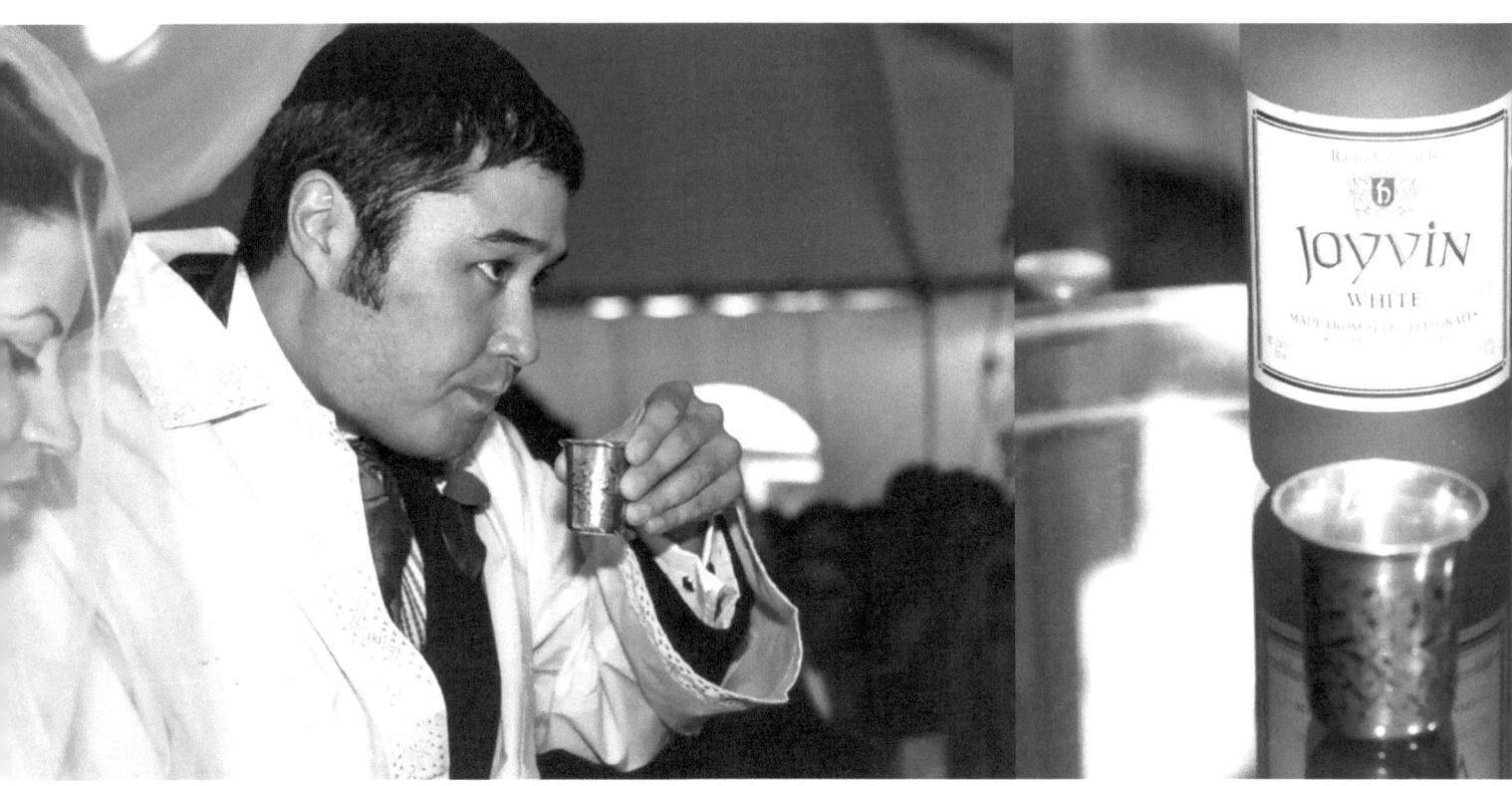

I once would have laughed at statements like, "Jews are paranoid. They bring it on themselves." I am Jew

Miller once said something like if Israel moved to Antarctica, anti-Semites would be there in snow suits.

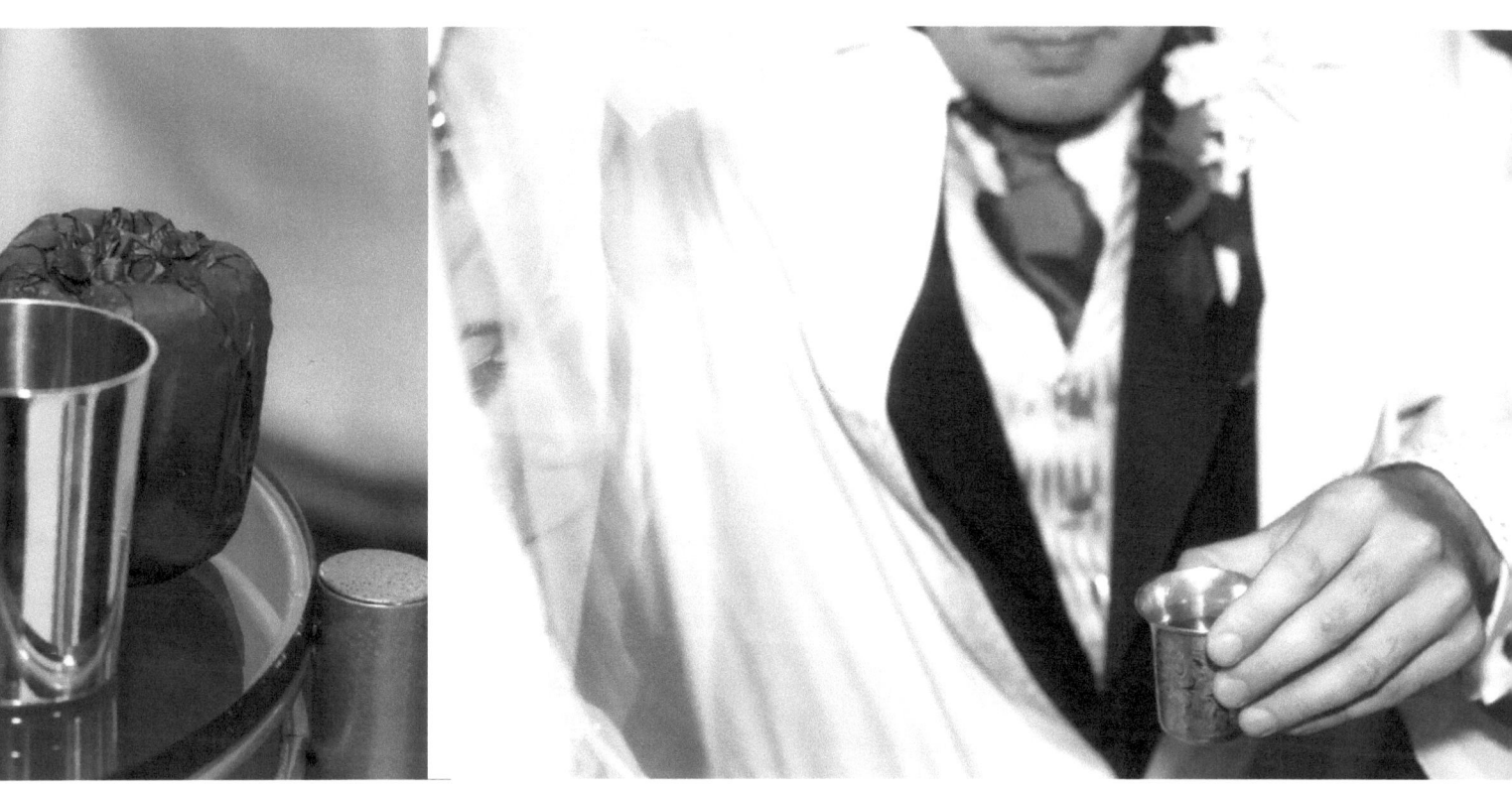

ish and, trust me, they bring it on us. The hate comes to me on the streets unprovoked and venomous.

"My cousin, Judy, and I were around nine when we began to hear little things, like grandfather's last name had been shortened (from Sottnekoff to Sottneck), things began to come out, but it was hushed. "Oh maybe he was Russian Orthodox." Total denial.

The kiddush cup came after my aunt, Margaret, was clearing out stuff after my grandfather's death. It was sent to me by Judy. I was told it was my grandfather's. He brought it with him.

I'm not even sure why I got it in the end, I wasn't sure what it was. But I eventually figured it out. The Judaism part of it, the link.

Jules' brother lived in Borough Park in Brooklyn. Jules' brother's son, when he got older, he started researching his family history. But the information out of Russia was scarce.

My Irish cousin Betty, my grandmother's cousin, well, she was very Catholic. At a wedding, my cousin who was researching the family was mentioning there was Jewish blood, and there may have been rabbis in the family. My cousin Betty reacted terribly saying "Oh my god" clutching her chest. "It couldn't be, it couldn't be!"

My grandfather, Jules', death was a big loss, a big void. Everything changed.

kaethe akira's mother

Akira's mother, Kaethe, with her grandfather, Jules

AVIVA — 84 YEARS OLD — DECEASED
BORN: RIGA, LATVIA

There was a message on my voicemail from Salvatore. He is the doorman of my client, Aviva. He is also a Power of Attorney, which means he was given legal permission by Aviva to take care of her financial matters and estate. He usually called to set up doctor's appointments, to discuss Medicare issues, or to inquire of any social events she might enjoy. This voicemail simply said, "Akira, she died."

She stopped breathing on a Saturday evening, right after the Jewish Sabbath ended. The home attendant called 911, but she could not be revived. While I am very sad, Aviva was suffering terribly. In the last six months, paranoia, delusions, and hallucinations began to become more apparent. She would call Salvatore at three in the morning screaming that the Nazis were coming; on the street she would think that police officers were the Gestapo; new visitors to her apartment were immediately suspect and part of some scheme to hurt her.

She was divorced and had no children or family. She needed assistance bathing, toileting, preparing food, and getting dressed. She used a wheelchair when she went outside. In the last months, she felt she had nothing to live for anymore. I believe she wanted a quiet that she had before the Nazis invaded her hometown and changed the course of her life forever.

Aviva was born in Riga, Latvia. Before World War II, there were 40,000 Jews in Riga. By the end of the War there were 150. Jews were interned in the Latvian ghetto. Like all ghettos, the conditions were deplorable. Basic freedoms were taken away and curfews kept Jews in prison-like conditions. Jews had to wear yellow stars, food was rationed, and many starved to death.

Soon after, the full-scale liquidation of Jews began.

Aviva remembers a cold march where Nazi soldiers asked, facetiously, "Why are you walking so fast? When you walk fast, the stragglers are shot. You are killing your own people."

When the marchers slowed down, they shot another Jew and said, "Move faster, you're going to slow."

She vividly remembers an "old woman with a club foot" who survived the march. She tells me this is the perfect example of self-preservation.

In late 1941, 26,000 Latvian Jews were marched into the Rumbula Forest on the outskirts of Riga, shot by German killing squads and buried in mass graves. When the Third Reich feared the mass graves would be found, they had Jews dig up the graves and burn the bodies. The Jews were then shot and burned themselves.

EVA, 74 YEARS OLD, HIDDEN CHILD
BORN: LODZ, POLAND

Eva left frantic calls on my voicemail over the weekend stating that she is going to die. Something about her doctor not being reachable.

The heat does something to her. It triggers no options. She demanded that we help her change doctors. Whenever Eva has a panic attack she tries to change all her associations.

I said, "So, you've been on the rampage?" She got very angry with me and said she wanted a new agency and a new social worker. I said, "Well, when you decide what you want to do, let me know." She hung up the phone.

During the Holocaust, Eva worked on a farm with her mother, on the outskirts of Bremen. They planted vegetables, and were on false papers.

The family was nice to them and they ate well. She worked with two young men in their early teens who always talked about sex and the girls they slept with. She says she would listen to these stories, but could not understand "sex."

One time a young man showed her his penis, she looked away. She tells me that she was never told about sex, and had to figure it out for the first time in an apartment on the Lower East Side, when she was in her early twenties. In hindsight, she knows that her mother had sex with the man who owned the farm so they would be sheltered and well-fed.

Eventually, she was separated from her mother by choice in case the Nazis came through. It was made to look like she was the daughter of the farmer. Many of the local older men would touch her. She always looked away and shut off that part of her brain.

When her mother came back, they made their way to a big city in Germany. They both worked in a factory making a thick, tough material to be used for linens. Normal materials were becoming scarce. Eva once decided to jam one of the sewing machines, and the daily operation was shut down for three hours.

She proudly says that it was her contribution to fighting the Nazis.

In 1940, the Nazis established a ghetto in Lodz. 200,000 Jews were crammed into a small neighborhood and forced to live in harsh conditions. Roughly 40,000 Jews died from unlivable conditions. 70,000 Jews were deported to the Chelmo extermination camp.

I get it now. I was on the other side once. I was a secular non-Jew. I knew of the Holocaust, anti-Semitism, and Israel through the lens of public school education and the media. Not that my education and the media didn't give me a somewhat accurate account. I knew that people hated Jews for just being Jews. I knew the Holocaust was a deplorable scar on humanity. I knew that Israel was a contentious piece of land, but I saw it from a distance. I intellectualized what Jews experienced. Outsiders can always say do this or that and the problem will be solved. But hating Jews is from time immemorial. It's encoded in our genes. It's in our everyday language. It's second nature. It's easy. And most importantly, it is surreptitiously condoned by governments, world leaders, and the United Nations. When you blame Israel for crimes against humanity tantamount to Hitler, there is no moral equivalence. The onus is always on Jews to change.

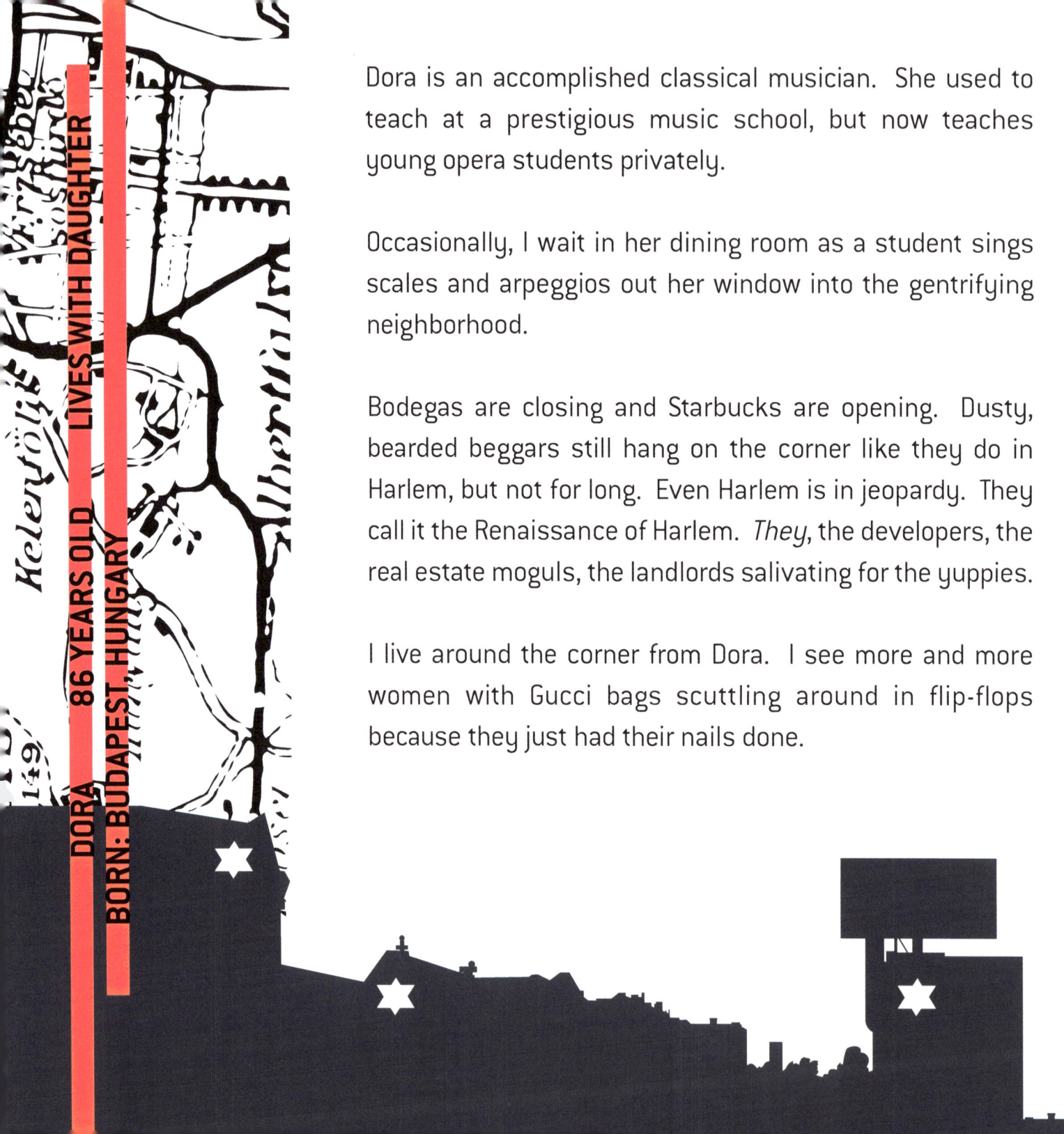

DORA • 86 YEARS OLD • LIVES WITH DAUGHTER • BORN: BUDAPEST, HUNGARY

Dora is an accomplished classical musician. She used to teach at a prestigious music school, but now teaches young opera students privately.

Occasionally, I wait in her dining room as a student sings scales and arpeggios out her window into the gentrifying neighborhood.

Bodegas are closing and Starbucks are opening. Dusty, bearded beggars still hang on the corner like they do in Harlem, but not for long. Even Harlem is in jeopardy. They call it the Renaissance of Harlem. *They*, the developers, the real estate moguls, the landlords salivating for the yuppies.

I live around the corner from Dora. I see more and more women with Gucci bags scuttling around in flip-flops because they just had their nails done.

Today, Dora needed help sorting out her medical bills. She has been in and out of the hospital for pneumonia and a bad fall. She has osteoarthritis and uses a walker when she goes outside.

Dora is ashamed to use the walker and says people get angry at her when she uses the electric bus lift.

While I am there, a guy calls and tells her she just won a lottery of $100,000.

He says she just has to send $1,200 for processing fees.

When she gives the phone to me, the guy hangs up. I tell her it's a scam and to never give money to people over the phone.

200,000 Jews lived in Budapest before World War II. The complicit Hungarian government forced Jews into a designated area and marked the buildings with Stars of David. 25,000 Hungarian Jews were deported to the Auschwitz-Birkenau extermination camp. 20,000 Jews were taken from the Jewish area, shot along the Danube, and thrown in the river.

PAULINE — 83 YEARS OLD — LIVES ALONE — BORN: BRUSSELS, BELGIUM

I meet Pauline at a bank on Park Avenue South and 28th Street. She doesn't trust her home attendants so she requests a third person present. But when she is home there is not a third person. The attendant, Nadine, is a nice woman, but angry with Pauline because she knows that Pauline accuses her of stealing. I have seen no evidence that the attendant steals money.

Pauline hides money around her apartment in envelopes with about 50 rubber bands around them. She will whisper to me where envelopes are hidden.

"Listen, there is one in this drawer, $100." "I have $2000 in a suitcase behind my raincoat in the closet."

Nadine can hear her. "I know you keep your money in that drawer and I haven't taken it yet," she yells from the kitchen, as she stirs something to a bubbly boil. But Nadine has stuck around longer than any attendant. Pauline has a history of going through attendants. They just don't want to put up with her accusations and demands. I tell her that she is lucky to have Nadine. She draws me in close and whispers, "Akira, you're still green. She is waiting for me to die so she can take all my money."

Pauline lives alone in a low-income building. She receives Medicaid and SSI. She was never married, and has no relatives left. In the apartment she uses a walker. When she goes outside, she uses a wheelchair. She is very frail. Less than 100 pounds. Her legs have open sores from poor nutrition. They are bandaged four times a week by a nurse.

At the bank she requests a money order to pay her rent. $195. She cashes a check from a charity organization for Holocaust survivors, and withdraws $300 for living expenses. $20 in quarters for the laundry. When the banker gives her fifties, she notices that one of the fifties looks different. It is a new printing, but she thinks it's counterfeit. "I read about it in the paper." She insists on an old fifty and the teller humorously obliges.

I tell her I will call her tomorrow. She says, "If I'm still alive." I say, "Oh, stop it, you will be." She laughs and says, "God willing."

On the outskirts of Brussels, in the town of Mechelen, the Nazis set up a transit camp. It was a strategic site, between Brussels and Antwerp, where most of the Jewish population lived. Mechelen also had a direct rail connection to the extermination camps. 25,000 Jews were deported to Auschwitz-Birkenau.

I'm just one Jew under the imperious weight of anti-Semitic world history. What can I do to change things? I grew up with none of the baggage of growing up Jewish, yet I'm starting to accumulate my own set of travel bags. I think the difference is that I grew up with a sense of not being persecuted.

So now when I am persecuted for being Jewish, my processes and reactions are not historic. Yes, I get upset, but I don't say, "This is how it is and this is how it will always be." My baggage is knowledge, not formative structures in my personality or psyche.

SARAH • 94 YEARS OLD
24-HOUR HOME ATTENDANT
BORN: VIENNA, AUSTRIA

Sarah has mid-stage dementia, and when I meet her she says, in a very lucid moment, "I'm going to die soon," with a big smile. And she means it. She doesn't remember that I met her once before, about two weeks ago when her daughter was in town.

Today we sit at the dining room table and play "Jumble." It's a word game in the Daily News. She uses scrabble-like word pieces made from paper with letters on them to help her put words together. She seems to be having difficulty with the first word.

URFOL
I give her a hint. "What do you bake a cake with?"
She says, "Flour?"
The second word jumble is SWEYN
She asks, "Who are you?" I say, "I'm a social worker."
NEWSY
The third word jumble is OBNIBB
She asks, "What do you do?" I say, "I'm a social worker."
BOBBIN

We look at pictures that she has arranged on her wall of family and friends. She has written the names of each family member and friend under each picture. This helps her remember who they are. Today she could not recognize her son. She kept saying it was her husband. The grandchildren she just gazed at, vacuously, and moved on to people she could recognize.

Sarah is positioned at the table and looks at me seriously, confoundedly.

Then her eyes light up like a revelation. She notices the Star of David around my neck. She touches it with her hand as if it holds some magical power. *"I'm Jewish, I'm Jewish," she says, excitedly.*

She has the Daily News opened. We continue to play Word Jumble.

HEMIC   Chime

FRIEVY   Verify

SPYDOR   Dropsy

In 1938, Vienna had a Jewish population of 170,000. The Austrian Republic was incorporated into Nazi Germany known as the Anschluss or "connection." Soon anti-Jewish legislation was installed in Vienna. Four years later, the population was 8,000.

I sat outside of Jewish Home and Hospital on 106th Street. I had a half hour before my next appointment with Judith, so I walked to Central Park West and sat on a bench. This is a sort of no-man's land, an area between 96th Street and 110th where pedestrians and traffic quiet down. The buildings look rundown, there are no more doormen loitering under awnings with regal names, checking out women in skirts, scuttling to taxis to get shiny paper shopping bags with cloth handles, filling the pewter dog bowl for thirsty pure-breeds.

Trash flutters in corners, a Frito-Lays bag entwined in leaves, a fossil of our times that anthropologists or aliens will find. Windows of grand stone facades are open and dark, no air conditioning, and you can just tell by an item or two in the window that these people are poor – a red votive candle with visage of Christ, a rusty fan propped with no regard as to whether it falls out, a man in an undershirt. Dirt and neglect coat these buildings.

Random men sit on far away benches, some are lying down, some have their shirt tied around their head, some shirtless, some skinny and lithe from drugs and no food. I see a black man hopping along demonstratively, talking, cursing, arms waving. I can tell by the distress of passer-bys that he is "crazy." People avoid him like opposing magnets, curving around him subtly so he doesn't notice their aversion, so he doesn't go into a harangue about racism and follow them for a block or two before another demon distracts him.

He stops about twenty yards from me, wobbly, like a drunk John Wayne in a showdown. He's skinny, but he stands in such a way that his belly protrudes. He uses his belly as ballast, but which direction he is trying to orient himself to is unknown. He's carrying a dirty sports bag. His sneakers look big and lacy, like they are 3 sizes too big for him. He wears a faded Burger King t-shirt. The motto reads, "Have it your way." He says, "Did you see two guys over there? They stole some kid's baseball cap, just took it from him."

"Oh, yeah, you just got here, everybody says 'I just got here!'" He sits on a bench along the park, affected by my response. He nods "No" repeatedly to himself. He blows out disgusted air. I pretend to go about my business. I futz with my cell phone.

A white young woman in stylish jogging apparel runs by. She is very fit and attractively muscular. She checks her watch. She gives an air of efficiency and practicality. Her life is in order, she has somewhere to be in an hour. Go home, shower, catch a cab, she'll make it just in time. She runs towards 96th Street. Down there you see people walking dogs, bikes crossing into the park, traffic, kids, strollers, balloons, a hot dog stand. Globalization still has boundaries. It's called poverty.

He yells at the woman. He stands up and looks over the wall into Central Park. He picks up a soda can, shakes it out and puts it in his bag. I get up and walk toward Jewish Home and Hospital. I smell a waft of urine. I feel like I do not belong here. Is this New York City? My question is answered as I wait for the light at 106th Street. A set of steep stairs lead into the park, over and through the granite formations. No parks department guys in green vans clean here. The steps are overgrown and full of emptiness. I look at a stone sign engraved on the wall. It reads: "Stranger's Gate."

Georg Simmel, in his 1908 essay "The Stranger," alluded to the historical plight of the wandering Jew. But more importantly, "The Stranger" talked about anyone from another culture or society defined by "otherness." He said, "The Stranger is an element of the group itself an element whose membership within the group involves both being outside it and confronting it."   The stranger crosses our path today and may or may not be here tomorrow. That is the "danger" and "fear" we perceive in strangers. The stranger brings his "otherness" into the host culture and roams freely within the "threatening" comfort we hold so dear. When we perceive "fear" and "danger" in "otherness" we automatically assign negative assumptions to "The Stranger."   The stranger is lacking what we have. The stranger is a threat that we believe will do catastrophic damage to our way of life. The behavior of one stranger is the behavior of all strangers from that group, criminalized or deemed immoral.

In 1862, the Central Park Board of Commissioners wanted to name the 18 entrances to the park as a way to give meaning and identity. The park designers, Calvert Vaux and Frederick Law Olmstead, imagined the park to be an escape from a growing urban city where each gate would welcome people of different backgrounds. At the time, only four gates were chiseled into the surrounding stone walls.

In 1999, the remaining 14 gates were completed.

Running clockwise around the park from Columbus Circle they are:

Merchants' Gate: Columbus Circle original
Women's Gate: Central Park West at West 72nd Street
Explorers' Gate: CPW at West 77th Street
Hunters' Gate: CPW at West 81st Street
Mariners' Gate: CPW at West 85th Street
All Saints' Gate: CPW at West 97th Street
Boys' Gate: CPW at West 100th Street
Strangers' Gate: CPW at West 106th Street
Warriors' Gate: Central Park North at Adam Clayton Powell Blvd. (7th Avenue)
Farmers' Gate: CPN at Malcolm X Blvd. (Lenox Ave.)
Pioneers' Gate: Duke Ellington/James Frawley Circle at 5th Avenue
Vanderbilt Gate (only gate named for a person): 5th Ave. at East 106th Street
Girls' Gate: 5th Avenue at East 102nd Street
Woodmen's Gate: 5th Avenue at East 96th Street
Engineers' Gate: 5th Avenue at East 90th Street
Inventors' Gate: 5th Avenue at East 72nd Street
Scholars' Gate: 5th Avenue at East 60th Street original
Artists' Gate: Central Park South at 6th Avenue original
Artisans' Gate: CPS at 7th Avenue original

But why "Stranger's Gate?" There seemed to be a history to this particular place as one of strangeness and transition like airports and bus depots. Places where unwanted people congregate. In a February 2, 2003 New York Times article titled "New York Observed; Portals to the 19th Century," Rebecca Chace made some great observations about how some of the gates still describe "life inside the walls."

Enter at the Children's gate on Fifth Avenue near 76th Street: there is a playground, and if you wander between this gate and Inventor's Gate at West 72nd Street you will see the statues of Alice in Wonderland and Hans Christian Anderson. There is a model boat pond to conquer if you can ship aboard a vessel heading out to sea. For the space of one's childhood, perhaps, it is possible to believe in growing up to become an inventor.

Opposite Merchant's Gate at Columbus Circle, it is eerily appropriate to see the new AOL Time Warner Center towering higher every day as a testament to the power of the American corporation. Stranger's Gate at 106th Street and Central Park makes an entrance opposite the building we thought was a haunted castle when I was growing up in the neighborhood.

In fact, it was a hospital, then a nursing home, and now, after years of neglect, it is being turned into a condominium. But the construction isn't complete, and with pigeons roosting in its four turrets, it still looks like an abandoned castle. A black slate stairway leads into the park at Stranger's Gate, and to enter the park there is to enter a fairy tale: a wilderness welcoming all strangers, as Olmsted and Vaux intended.

I noticed the menacing Castle that has been gutted and romantically marketed to millionaires. I saw the sign out front with price tags reaching 25 million bucks. I noticed the high pointy gates to protect the future inhabitants. Rebecca Chace reported that there were early plans to erect high iron gates instead of the low walls and unassuming entrances you see today so high society could be reminded of "their place in the world," but this plan never came to be because Olmsted vehemently opposed such gates as a barrier to the symbol of democracy.

Judith fell a few weeks ago and came to Jewish Home and Hospital for rehabilitation. She is a Holocaust survivor from Warsaw, Poland, who lost most of her family in Nazi

The stranger is a threat that we believe will do catastrophic damage to our way of life.

concentration camps — a perfect example of the extremes of stranger-fear.

When I arrived Judith was just leaving for occupational therapy. She invited me to come along. She was escorted by wheelchair through a busy maze of stretchers, wheelchairs, doctors, maintenance men in blue, social workers, nurses, and administrators. The facility is old in sections, wood-paneling, convulsing ventilation systems, donor lists of dead people on tarnished metal plaques - reminders of their place in the world.

The therapy room was filled with strengthening equipment: a circular arm crank, overhead pulleys for arm strengthening, a semi-circle hoop that had colored rings attached to move back and forth, and a mock kitchen to practice activities of daily living. Most of the older people in the room were despondent. Some slumped, others groaned. Therapists spoke loudly and discreetly to maximize communication. Encouraging words seemed bathetic. "Good, Mr. Dickson, good job." "Elsa, you're such a strong woman."

A religious Jewish woman named Malka introduced herself to me. She has been working with Judith since she arrived. Judith proudly introduced me as her social worker like a doting grandmother. I sit at the mock kitchen table and Judith is escorted to the arm crank machine. She does this for 5 minutes. Malka puts a chair behind her in case she falls backwards. They talk quietly and I can only hear bits and pieces of the conversation as nurses and therapists scurry in and out of the therapy room yelling questions, personal jokes, looking for something and leaving quickly to a minor emergency or doctor's request. "Where are you going for vacation, Christine?" "Does anybody know where the bigger walker is?"

Judith is escorted to the kitchen next. Today, they decide that Judith will prepare tea for us. Malka and Judith work on positioning her walker next to the counter. She tells Judith, "Never use the front burners. Always use the back burners, this way you can't burn yourself." Judith is told to hold onto the counter. She works her way to the kitchen sink and begins to fill the teakettle.

"Remember, you need water for three people," says Malka.

The kettle starts to get heavier and Judith's arm drops in large increments. "Okay, that's enough," says Malka. Malka turns the faucet off.

Judith tries to carry the kettle, but Malka says, "Use the counters, that's what they're there for." Judith slides the kettle onto a back burner, and they turn on the gas together. Judith turns to me and says, "Welcome to Judith's Tea Party." She giggles.

There seemed to be a history to this particular place as one of strangeness and transition like airports and bus depots. Places where unwanted people congregate.

I walked down to 99th and Broadway for my next home-visit. It's warm out. Latino men sit on stoops and car hoods. They yell up to neighbors or family members in open windows with no screens. Someone comes to the window, they talk in Spanish, and the men on the stoop laugh. This was the neighborhood on 99th and Broadway a few years ago. The neighborhood is gentrifying. Bodegas, 99-cent stores, and laundromats are giving way to Starbucks, sidewalk cafes, and designer clothing stores. Low-income SROs still show the old neighborhood as toothless tenants smoke out front, coughing, talking loudly, toenails unclipped and discolored. But, then the middle-class pedestrian becomes the norm, baguettes sticking out of shopping bags.

Gristede's between 99th and 100th Street was recently closed and torn down. A big development company is building two 30-story luxury condos. Upper West Side liberals came out of the woodwork, protesting greedy development. They argued that the integrity of the neighborhood would be lost. What about the Latinos who have moved further uptown when their rents were tripled, then gutted, remodeled, and rented to Upper West Side liberals and 20-year-old rich kids from Columbia?

Everything is relative.

SAUL — 80 YEARS OLD — LIVES ALONE
BORN: ANTWERP, BELGIUM

Saul lives on 45th Street between 5th and 6th Avenues. If you look closely the buildings hint of a time gone by when buildings were low, when family names were engraved just below the top crown. Slowly, the past is being enveloped by skyscrapers, a hodge-podge of garish signs, logos, fonts, flags, banners, grand-opening silk, neon, arrows, lights, upstairs, downstairs, buzzers, fighting for more and more space within a finite space. Old buildings are getting quick-fix face lifts, slap some cement over brick-work, nail metal sheets across rotting wood, cover, hide, make new again, just for a little while so quick money can be made and then get out, letting the empty, cluttered space, be window-soaped until another cell-phone joint, nail shop, or deli pops up for a little while.

Old people in rent-controlled apartments are still scattered in these commercial areas as voracious landlords wait for their deaths. Sell the precarious brick buildings to developers to tear down to put up glass towers with stainless steel kitchens, gym, pool, marble lobby, garage for black shiny sports car, wife with D & G emblazoned wardrobe.

Left-wing Westsiders in Birkenstocks with graying hair and

baby-boomer ideologies cannot stop progress. Yes, they'll win a battle or two, save a building from becoming a chain-store, but in the end progress prevails. The turn of your time and your worldview gives way to the next generation in line.

Saul lives on the third floor above a Spanish beauty salon, above a sketchy office with names with single letters with periods after them. Some degree or qualification or certification. How qualified are you if you're hunkered down in a wood-paneled hell-hole, dirty ashtrays full of accordioned cigarette butts, yelling into the phone, a jai-alai-basket-nailed secretary talking to her girlfriend on another line and chewing gum, fat, sweaty loose-tied men coughing, mucus gurgling, expectorating in the garbage basket? What are these guys selling or buying or forcing from people?

I knock on Saul's door. It takes him a minute to answer the door. Locks click, chains unlatch, he peeks out, recognizes me and then opens the door wide. He gestures me in and I begin to talk to him. He motions for me to be quiet until we get deeper into his small studio apartment. He reverses the process and secures the door behind me. Once he is behind

In 1940, the Nazis established the Breendonk detention camp on the outskirts of Antwerp. Many Belgian resistance fighters were held at Breendonk. Jews were detained temporarily, then shipped to Michelen and then ultimately to Auschwitz-Birkenau.

his desk he says hello. I remind myself to ask him about this. He seems paranoid to me.

I have to maneuver through small aisles surrounded by years of clutter. His work area behind his desk is the only sign of life. Where he works there is no dust. Everything else in the room is dusty, sticky, stuck together, bookbinding glue oozed and dry, sun-faded posters, books, curtains, window edges putty-cracked like a desert floor, Cup-O-Noodle Styrofoam containers stacked, counting his days in processed meals, dried diarrhea down the side of the toilet.

He gets into it about his restitution claim, about his father's house and property that was looted and stolen in Belgium during the war. I had spoken to him about a month and a half ago and he told me a decision had been made. I had contact by email with Brussels about his claims and they informed me that he would be notified by mail. Saul shows me the letter. It turns out they are giving him 13,900 euros, about $17,000. He has not sent back the requested information so arrangements can be made to transfer the payment to his account.

He tells me that he wants to appeal the decision because

they rejected his claim about his father's house. Their decision states that there was not sufficient evidence to support his claim. He asks about lawyers and suing the committee in Brussels. I tell him that if he appeals the decision it will probably take another two years before they come up with a decision, and, in that time, he would not get the $17,000. My advice to him is that he accept the payment and then look into appeals later. I know that he has been obsessed with this matter for over two years and in some ways he enjoys keeping busy with the paper work, phone calls to his lawyer, and looking into matters of foreign government policies and laws. It has made him feel productive, active, involved.

To: indemnification commission for the
Belgian Jewish Community's Assets
16 rue de la loi
1000 Brussels, Belgium

Description of assets as complete as possible:

Oriental carpets, large sizes - in the dining room - the living room - the library, bedroom + the master bedroom

Smaller oriental rugs in the lone corridors – from the entrance of the apartment to the maid's room – to the entrance of the kitchen and dining room – and on to both bedroom entrances.

Dining room

large dining table

many upholstered chairs

credenza and large tall buffet

2 large fauteuils drapes on windows

chandeliers on ceiling

Royal Doulton Server

Wedgewood Server

Sterling Silverware

fine China

Crystal

Porcelain

Living room

piano

tall RCA phonograph with impressive
record collection - several arm chairs
"fauteuils" drapes on windows
chandeliers on ceiling

Library

desk and chair

large armoire "bibliotheque"

with collection of classical books

smaller armoire with additional books

stamp collection

drapes on window -

two fauteuils

ceiling chandelier.

Candelabras

Bedroom

two armoires

2 beds

two chests of drawers

clothing

linens

drapes on windows

modest lighting on ceiling.

Master bedroom - more elaborate

2 armoires

two chests of drawers

two beds

drapes on windows

chandelier from ceiling

clothing

fur coats

linens.

Kitchen

many cupboards -

extensive cookware

1940 standard equipment

THE SCOTCH-TAPED MEZUZAH

Gertrude lives in a senior housing facility on the Upper West Side. It's really just independent apartments with a social work office in the lobby and cheaper rent.

She is an 80-year old Holocaust survivor from Warsaw. When I visited her for the first time, her apartment had no furniture except a couch, table and one chair. Garbage and personal belongings were scattered about the apartment like a ransacked Jewish home during the Nazi regime. She has been living out of her bags since she moved in six months ago. Her two sons, one ten blocks away and another living in Brooklyn, have not been over to see her squalid living conditions.

Dirty pans and dishes lay in the sink. Underwear and bras hang from the shower curtain rod. She does her laundry in her small bathroom sink to save money. She goes to a local Jewish organization for one-dollar lunches everyday. Sometimes she tells me they give her an extra lunch to take home for dinner.

Out her living room window is a courtyard with trees, patios, lawn chairs, and barbeques. The apartments across the courtyard are going for a million. Her windows have no shades and at night people can see into her apartment, where she sleeps on a couch or sits by the open window to get some cool air.

I notice that she paces when she talks and I can picture yuppies watching her pace the apartment, talking out loud to herself about how she is going to turn her life around.

Turning her life around is all she talks about. What she forgets is that she has been trying to turn her life around since the war and she is no less frantic and desperate than she was when she was a little girl in Warsaw, hiding in an underground bunker from the Nazis.

She lost her parents in concentration camps. She survived with her sister and brother and made it to the United States. She married a fellow survivor, also from Warsaw, and had two sons. Her marriage was filled with emotional and physical abuse. She told stories and showed scars on her legs where he threw coffee mugs, a menorah, a lamp, a hard-covered siddur, "whatever he could find."

She says he slept around. "The boys saw everything."

She talks of her son Yosef, the youngest one, who lives alone in a basement apartment in Brooklyn. He's in his fifties, single, no job, and living on SSI. He has many health problems and she says, "He got his father." She worries the most about Yosef and says "nebuch" (pity) when she thinks of him never marrying and raising a family.

Her oldest son, Aaron is married with no children. He lives with his wife in a studio apartment on the Upper West Side. Gertrude was there until six months ago when her wait-listed senior apartment application came through after three years.

I spoke with Aaron on the phone and there is a palpable anxiousness. He's frenetic, interrupting me and then apologizing, but then doing it again, over and over. He must tell me everything in detail, while filling me in on the injustices of the world. But, he advocates for his mother. He wants her to get more money "that she rightfully deserves."

He knew nothing about her present living conditions, which is very telling about how supportive he has been. When I tell him how she has been living, he acknowledges it matter-of-factly and says he will get over to the apartment. His wife cuts in on the phone conversation and starts yelling, "Aaron, I told you, I told you, you must go over there." They yell back and forth before I interrupt to get back to the issue of Gertrude.

The wife talks to me in the same way, as if she has to get everything out that has been held in for decades, as if she will never talk to me again, as if it is appropriate to lay all your issues out for a complete stranger. There are two-dozen issues that have to be fixed, some theirs, but they can't focus on one long enough for me to tell them how we should proceed. Everything is spilled out, except their marital issues, which are apparent.

Slowly, I have been helping Gertrude get her apartment in order. I contacted the social worker in her housing facility and they have set up a housekeeper to clean her apartment twice a month. Gertrude never went to the social workers in the building because she thought they were in cahoots with the landlord, who, in essence, is a "Nazi." Her rent is $800 a month, which is equivalent to most rent controlled apartments, but her income is only $1400 a month. She gets about $800 from Social Security and $600 from Germany restitution. She must live on $600 dollars a month.

This is poverty. This is what many older people are facing in America today.

She now gets kosher Meals On Wheels from a Jewish agency in the city, and I am applying to a Holocaust agency for monthly financial assistance in the amount of $150 per month. We are applying for a reduced-fare metro card and a Medicare savings program that would waive her monthly Medicare expense. Our agency is buying her orthopedic shoes for her arthritic feet. Her son Aaron came over and forced his mother to put things in order. He had a laundry service clean her clothes and linens, and he bought her an air conditioner for the summer.

Gertrude is out of crisis-mode physically, but mentally it's as if nothing has changed. She calls me most mornings, and leaves messages about minutiae. The world is still closing in on a daily basis. She cries about Yosef. She cries about how her husband damaged "the children." Anger pokes through at times and she slams her blue-veined fist on the table, the focused energy that saved her from the Nazis.

"I would run in the streets looking for the bunker, instead of staying home with him." She tells me that her husband beat her so much that once, in a delusional state, she was searching for the underground bunker in Poland where she hid from the Nazis. Things were so bad that she wanted to go back to that place.

In some ways, she still lives as if she is in a bunker. The world outside is noisy, dangerous, evil, and not to be trusted. Nazis lurk in supermarket checkout lines, in the social work office of her building, even at the JCC. She keeps her important papers, documents, bills, bank statements close-by, folded and worn. She can reach for them at anytime. Money is kept in her bra, just in case.

The bunker was a womb. A dark, closed environment, but safe. The bunker saved her life and she continues to seek the bunker in all her daily doings. Even so, I find her amazing. With all her difficulties, she struggles to make ends meet and hopes for a better life. She still keeps kosher, she reads her siddur every day, and she cries for her children "like a good Jewish mother" - that's what I tell her.

When I first saw the scotch-taped mezuzah on her front door, it epitomized the chaos and disarray of her life. When I got to know her it made sense that she would tape a mezuzah to the door, instead of taking the time to properly screw it in, like most of her Jewish neighbors.

It made sense that she was living out of bags and neglecting garbage and dirty dishes. When you're in survival mode constantly, the every day stuff just doesn't matter. Moving, running, hiding is all one thinks about.

However irrational her fears may be at times, Gertrude shows courage and strength.

With all her fears and her devastating past, she can still say that she is a Jew loud and clear, but, just in case, she can pull down the mezuzah, grab her bags, have her money and documents ready, and escape to safety. For her, safety is always the next place, which is the last place, which is ultimately the dark closed bunker she will never find.

It epitomized the chaos and disarray of her life...When you're in survival mode constantly, the every day stuff just doesn't matter.

MOVING, RUNNING, HIDING IS ALL ONE THINKS ABOUT.

On 21 Heshvan 5767, exactly 8 days ago today, Ellie and I fulfilled one of God's most important commandments: "Be fruitful and multiply."

When I think of this God-given commandment, for me, it is all about Jewish survival. As you know I am a convert to Judaism – 3 in Jewish years – not much older than my new son, Boaz Jules, who is exactly 8 days old today. While we are both Jews, he had the privilege of being born Jewish. I find that many born Jews take their Judaism for granted. For all of you who know Ellie and me, it was a long and difficult journey to get to this wonderful moment we are celebrating today.

The Talmud says, "Where you are supposed to go, your feet will take you." Today, I am truly home as a Jew. But the funny thing is that I never really left home. I have Jewish blood coursing through my veins.

My great-grandfather, Jules Sottnekoff, came to America at the turn of the 20th century to escape the Tsarist pogroms of Russia. He shortened his name to Sottnek when he entered Ellis Island in 1911. He hid his Jewishness from the family, and chose to never speak about it.

He didn't want to subject his family to the violent anti-

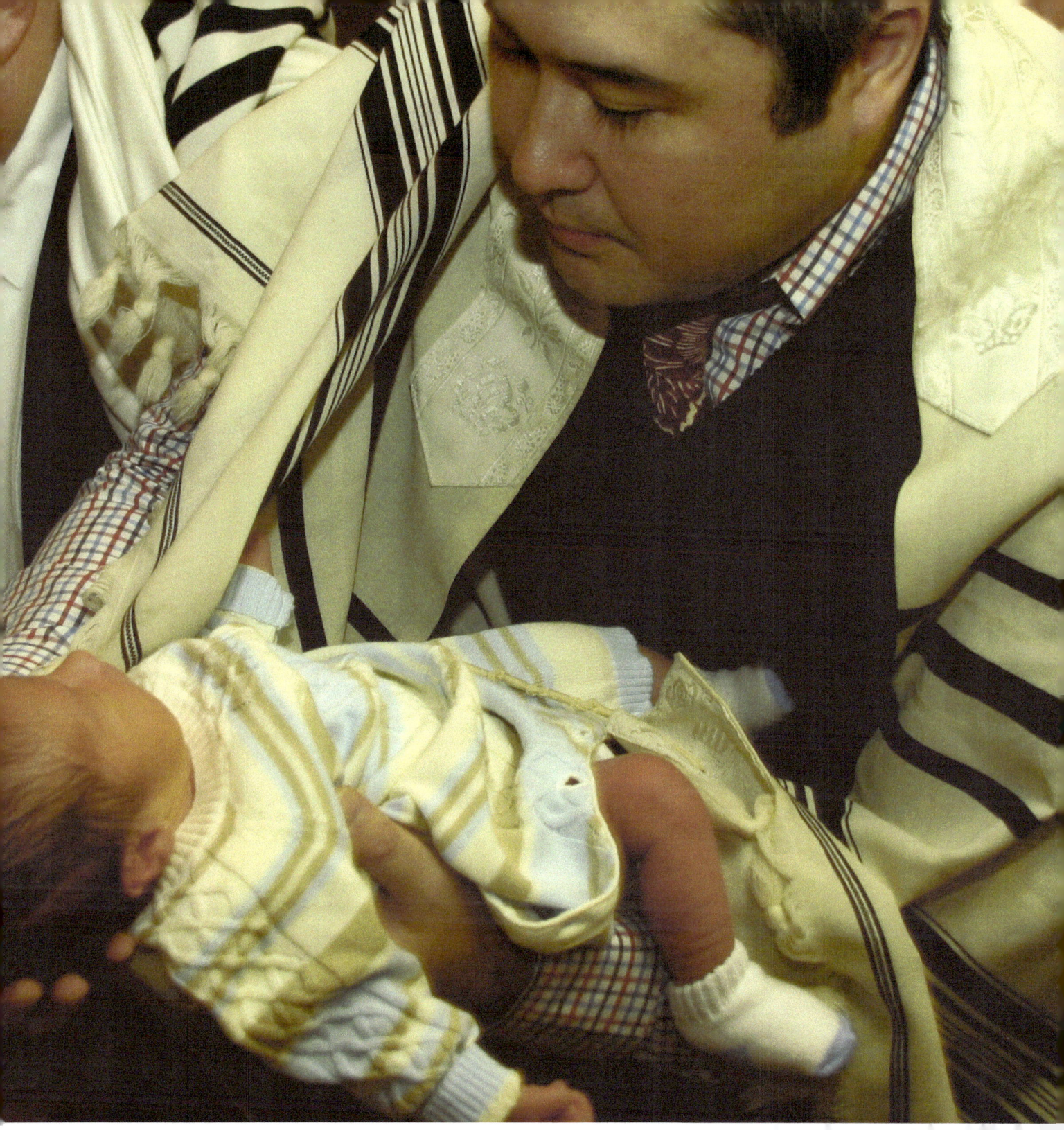

Semitism that he experienced in Riga, Latvia. In a way, he was trying to protect his family, but in another way, he was denying his family their true identity.

I've learned that silence does not lead to good things for Jews.

Under our chuppah two years ago, I drank from my great-grandfather's Kiddush cup, one of the few items he chose to take with him in hopes of a better life. The Kiddush cup sat in a Brooklyn basement until, finally, it ended up in the hands of his great-grandson 93 years later.

Me, his Jewish great-grandson.

Two years later, Ellie and I have given birth to Boaz Jules. His first name is for the husband of Ruth, the famous Jewish convert. Throughout my Jewish studies and conversion to Judaism, I was always struck by her timeless simple words that spoke so much about how I felt:

For whither though goest I will go, thy people thall by my people and thy God, my God.

So simple, yet so profound for those privileged enough to experience it's declaration.

My son's middle name is an homage to my great-grandfather who hid his Judaism to protect his family, yet, ironically, is the link that has brought Judaism back to his family. In some ways, I believe he knew the Kiddush cup would be discovered one day.

Without Jules' hope for a better world, my son and I would never have been born.

If my Japanese father, who was a small boy in Hirohito's Japan during World War II, can sit next to Ellie's Zaydie, a Holocaust escapee from Hungary, at our wedding 60 years after the Holocaust, then anything is possible. If my Japanese relatives can eat gefilte fish with chopsticks at my aufruf, then our world has hope.

As a Jew, I will teach Boaz well – to be a proud Jew, never to be silent, and to never take his Judaism for granted.

I know this as a Jew-by-choice who was not always accepted by Jews, yet wanted to be a Jew with all my heart and soul.

Most, importantly, I will teach Boaz Jules that Jewish survival is up to us.

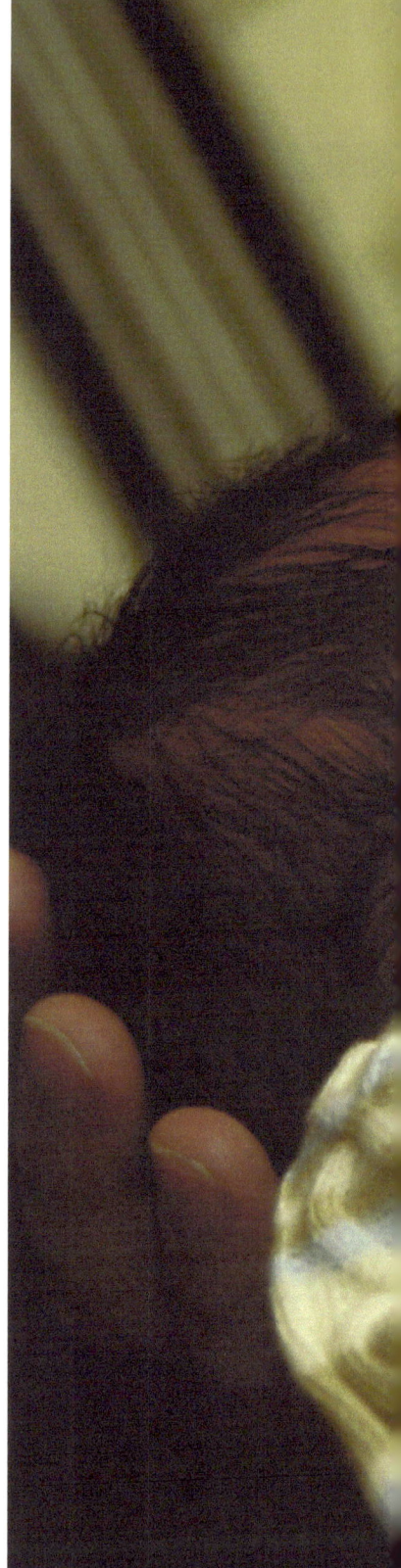

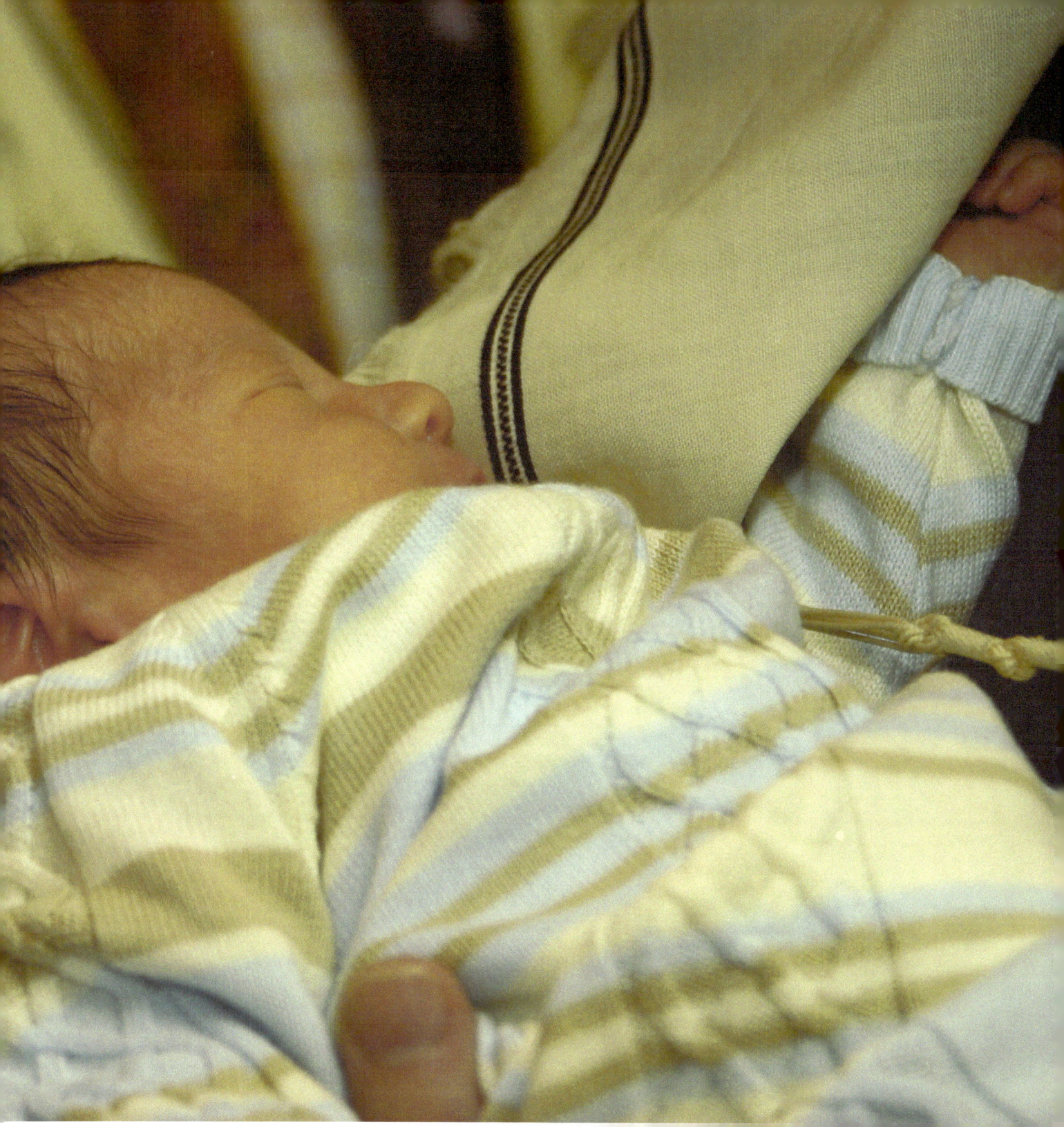

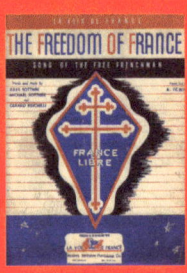

Ellie Ohiso and Akira Ohiso live in New York City with their son, Boaz. *Surviving* is their first book.

www.ingramcontent.com/pod-product-compliance
Lightning Source LLC
Chambersburg PA
CBHW041531220426
43672CB00002B/7